This notebook belongs to:

Top 5 tips to efficiently learn any foreign language

1. Learn from context

If you learn single words, you will be never able to speak any language fluently. Context-based learning will help your brain to pronounce a whole sentence without long and unnatural pauses.

What's more, by using this tip, you will avoid creating weird phrases and word connections that do not really exist in the world of native speakers. It helps you both to express yourself more efficiently and to improve your comprehension. You don't need to know all the words as long as you know the context of the sentence.

2. Listen and speak

Do newborns learn how to read first? Why are there people who manage without reading?

The first function of languages is communication and many people forget it. It all depends on the reason you learn a language, but for most cases, it's oral skills that make a difference. It feels shameful if you study a language for years using many books but you can't even order a pizza when you're abroad.

The reason why we prefer learning a foreign language by reading and writing is safety. When you have to speak to another human being, you are going out of your comfort zone and thus, you are more afraid of making mistakes. You should keep in mind that learning by speaking and listening is way more fun since you can watch films or speak with your foreign friends!

3. Learn what you need

Do you really learn a language to make speeches on global warming or endangered species of the Amazon rainforests? Don't you think it would be a better idea to know how to book a table for two people or be able to talk about your hobbies and occupation?

Each time you see an unknown word, ask yourself, "am I actually going to use it?" It all depends on the reason you choose to learn a language. If it's all about a two-week trip, just learn the basics to ask for direction or to buy bus tickets. If you're an engineer and you are going to use a language at work, focus on vocabulary you use daily when working.

Our brain has a limited capacity, so why do we learn words we are never going to use?

4. Reduce grammar lessons

Do newborns do grammar exercises before they speak? No, they simply learn it naturally with time. It's useful to be aware of some language structures and patterns which help you to become fluent faster, but grammar lessons should be nothing but additional value to your learning process.

Are grammar rules really necessary to convey your message the person you are conversing with?

5. It's all about repetition

Regularity is the key to success they say, and they are actually right. Our brain needs constant stimulation to store new expressions in long-term memory. It's better to have a 15 minute repetition on a daily basis than spending hours on learning once a month.

Good luck!

My current level of Spanish

....

My goal

....

Time to achieve my goal

....

The Spanish Alphabet - el alfabeto español

Letter	Spanish	Pronunciation
a	a	like the **a** in "father"
b	be	like the English **b** but pronounced very softly
c	ce	before a, o, u, like the **c** in "can"; before e, i, like the **c** in "cent"
ch	che	like the **ch** in "church"
d	de	like **d** in "bed" but with tongue forward, almost like **th** in "the"
e	e	like the **ay** in "pay"
f	efe	like the English **f**
g	ge	before a, o, u, like **g** in "get"; before e, i, like an English **h**
h	hache	always silent
i	i	like **ee** in "feet"
j	jota	like the English **h**
k	ka	like the English **k**
l	ele	like the English **l**
ll	elle	like the **y** in "yes"
m	eme	like the English **m**
n	ene	like the English **n**
ñ	eñe	like the **ny** in "canyon"
o	o	like the **o** in "no"
p	pe	like the English **p**
q	cu	like the English **k**
r	ere	like the English **r** but softer, almost sounds like a **d**
rr	erre	strongly trilled
s	ese	like the English **s**
t	te	like the English **t**
u	u	like the **oo** in "pool"
v	uve	almost no difference between **b** and **v** in Spanish
w	uve doble	like the English **w**
x	equis	like the English **x**
y	ye	like the English **y**; like **ee** in "tree" when used alone
z	zeta	like the English **s**

*Algo es algo,
menos es nada.*

*Something is something,
less is nothing.
(It's better than nothing.
Half a loaf is better than none.)*

El hábito no hace
al monje

The habit doesn't make the monk.
(Clothes do not make the man.)

Dame pan y dime tonto.

Give me bread and call me a fool.
(Think of me what you will.
As long as I get what I want,
it doesn't matter what you think.)

A los tontos no les dura el dinero.

*Money does not last for fools.
(A fool and his money
are soon parted.)*

Al mejor escribano se le va un borrón.

To the best scribe comes a smudge. (Even the best of us make mistakes. Nobody's perfect.)

A lo hecho, pecho.

To what is done, the chest.
(Face up to what is.
What is done is done.)

Glossary - the 100 most commonly spoken Spanish words

Spanish	English
como	as
I	I
su	his
que	that
él	he
era	was
para	for
en	on
son	are
con	with
ellos	they
ser	be
en	at
uno	one
tener	have
este	this
desde	from
por	by
caliente	hot
palabra	word
pero	but
qué	what
algunos	some

es	is
lo	it
usted	you
o	or
tenido	had
la	the
de	of
a	to
y	and
un	a
en	in
nos	we
lata	can
fuera	out
otros	other
eran	were
que	which
hacer	do
su	their
tiempo	time
si	if
lo hará	will
cómo	how
dicho	said
un	an
cada	each
decir	tell
hace	does
conjunto	set

tres	three
querer	want
aire	air
así	well
también	also
jugar	play
pequeño	small
fin	end
poner	put
casa	home
leer	read
mano	hand
puerto	port
grande	large
deletrear	spell
añadir	add
incluso	even
tierra	land
aquí	here
debe	must
grande	big
alto	high
tal	such
siga	follow
acto	act
por qué	why
preguntar	ask
hombres	men

cambio	change
se fue	went
luz	light
tipo	kind
fuera	off
necesitará	need
casa	house
imagen	picture
tratar	try
nosotros	us
de nuevo	again
animal	animal
punto	point
madre	mother
mundo	world
cerca	near
construir	build
auto	self
tierra	earth
padre	father

Enjoying this notebook?

As we are a small family company, your feedback is highly appreciated and important to us and we would be incredibly grateful if you could take a couple of minutes to leave a quick review.

Many thanks!

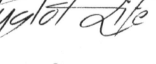

Made in the USA
Las Vegas, NV
15 July 2023

74757960R00066